Vegan Dinner

Other cookery books by Linda Majzlik published by Jon Carpenter

Vegan Dinner Parties

Linda Majzlik

Illustrated by Mark Blanford

JON CARPENTER

Our books may be ordered from bookshops or (post free) from
Jon Carpenter Publishing, Alder House, Market Street, Charlbury, OX7 3PH

Please send for our free catalogue

Credit card orders should be phoned or faxed to 01689 870437
or 01608 811969

Jon Carpenter Publishing
Alder House, Market Street, Charlbury, Oxfordshire OX7 3PH
☎ 01608 811969

First published 1999, reprinted 2002

ISBN 1 897766 46 7

Printed in England by J. W. Arrowsmith Ltd., Bristol BS3 2NT

Foreword by Juliet Gellatley

Juliet Gellatley is the founder and director of Viva!
(Vegetarians International Voice for Animals).

If you can remember back a decade or so, it was a very different world we inhabited then. It wasn't that easy to be vegetarian, let alone vegan. Gradually, the words 'vegetarian choice' sneaked quietly on to menus, first in the big cities and then throughout the land. Those of us involved in day to day campaigning to save animals have always been looking for revolution but what we have been faced with, perhaps even achieved, is evolution.

Part of that has been the acceptance of vegetarianism as mainstream. Now we have a similar battle on our hands with veganism and books such as this can only help and are to be truly welcomed — not least because the recipes are absolutely great.

Viva! is clear that vegetarianism and veganism are both steps along the same road and the important thing is to get people to begin the journey. Once they have, a process of enquiry starts which inevitably leads to a realisation of the inherent cruelty involved in the dairy industry. To discover that there is food after dairy — good, tasty, healthy, colourful, fresh food — is an important part of the progress towards a cruelty-free diet.

It often feels that as a people we are unbelievably slow to act when we know there is such cruelty involved in farming. Part of the reason is that we are trying to change entrenched attitudes which have little scientific basis. Take health, for example. On a regular basis, articles and comment appears in the Press and on TV which pretend to outline the pitfalls of vegetarian — and particularly vegan — diets. You know the kind of thing, an increased risk of everything from anaemia to marital breakdown.

The truth is very different and a meat-free diet is one of the healthiest possible. A meat *and* dairy free diet IS the healthiest possible. But try and get anyone to print that, despite the unanimity of such eminent health advisory bodies as the World Health Organisation, the American Dietetic Association, the British Medical Association and others.

If Viva! obtains actual footage of how meat is obtained — as we have done with pig farming and kangaroo killing amongst others — the media declines to show it because it's too horrific. It's fine to carry adverts for products which involve abysmal cruelty but you mustn't provide people with the information to make informed choices about those adverts. With the cards stacked so heavily against us, it's surprising that we achieve the successes we do.

Despite this, Viva! will continue to look for and work towards the elusive revolution. It will continue to sow the seeds for a more compassionate world — a vegan world. And to do that it needs all the help it can get. The 'normalisation' of veganism and vegan cooking is part of the process which is why this book is so important, particularly when written by such an eminent cookery writer as Linda Majzlik. For the sake of the world, its people and its animals, it is important to reclaim our food from those who pretend that pain and suffering are an essential part of our diet. They aren't.

Enjoy these great recipes because they strike a blow for the oppressed of the world — humans and animals alike.

For free information on any aspect of veganism, contact Viva!, 12 Queen Square, Brighton BN1 3FD. Tel 01273 777688.

An information pack is also available from the Vegan Society, 7 Battle Road, St Leonards on Sea TN37 7AA. Tel 01424 427393.

Introduction

This book suggests a festive vegan menu for each month of the year, all consisting of starter, main course and dessert. Of course these combinations are my personal choice, and it is up to you to choose what you want to serve for your own occasion, whether it is a formal dinner party, a wedding breakfast, or simply a get-together with friends. The index at the end of the book will help you find the dishes you are looking for. And if you need a pretext for a party, each month has some suggestions!

As a general rule, you will want a starter which complements, and is a light, mouth-watering appetizer for, the main course. The main course itself will be served with a choice of vegetables, prepared either in the traditional or a more unusual way, and accompanied by sauces and relishes to give that extra little touch of colour and flavour. And what could be better than rounding off your meal with a really sumptuous dessert?

Most of the recipes are for four people. If they are not, this is mentioned. You should have no problems finding the ingredients in health food shops and supermarkets.

Happy eating!

Linda Majzlik
Swanton Morley, 1998

JANUARY

Plan a feast for

New Year's Day (January 1)

Martin Luther King's Birthday
(USA: January 15, but date of holiday varies)

New Year's Dinner

Chinese leaf and fruit cocktail

•

*Buckwheat and bulgar loaf with mushroom
and brazil nut filling*

Crunchy sesame potato bake

Cauliflower in almond sauce

Brussels sprouts with chestnuts

Cranberry and apple sauce

•

Mincemeat, apple and almond charlottes

Chinese leaf and fruit cocktail *Serves 4/6*

8oz / 225g Chinese leaves, shredded

3oz / 75g black grapes, quartered

1oz / 25g sultanas

1oz / 25g raisins

2 kiwi fruits, peeled and chopped

2 eating apples, peeled, cored and chopped

4 dessert dates, stoned and chopped

1/2 oz / 15g pumpkin seeds

1 teaspoon coriander seeds, crushed

2 dessertspoons fresh fruit juice

1 dessertspoon white wine vinegar

1 dessertspoon sunflower oil

Combine the Chinese leaves, fresh and dried fruits and seeds in a large bowl. Mix the fruit juice with the vinegar and sunflower oil, pour over the salad and toss well. Serve in small bowls.

Buckwheat and bulgar loaf with mushroom and brazil nut filling

loaf

4oz / 100g roasted buckwheat

4oz / 100g carrot, scraped and grated

2oz / 50g bulgar wheat

2oz / 50g fresh wholemeal breadcrumbs

1oz / 25g soya flour

10 fl.oz / 300ml cold water

5 fl.oz / 150ml boiling water

1 small onion, peeled and finely chopped

1 celery stick, trimmed and finely chopped

1 dessertspoon sunflower oil

1 dessertspoon soy sauce

1 rounded teaspoon yeast extract

1 rounded teaspoon parsley

1 rounded teaspoon thyme

black pepper

filling

4oz / 100g mushrooms, wiped and finely chopped

4oz / 100g brazil nuts, finely grated

1 small onion, peeled and finely chopped

1 dessertspoon sunflower oil

1 teaspoon chives

black pepper

Put the buckwheat in a saucepan with the cold water and soy sauce. Bring to the boil, cover and simmer gently for about 10 minutes until the liquid has been absorbed. Remove from the heat. Dissolve the yeast extract in the boiling water and add the bulgar wheat. Cover and leave for 15 minutes. Drain the bulgar in a fine sieve over a bowl, pressing out as much liquid as possible with the back of a spoon. Keep the liquid and add the bulgar to the buckwheat. Heat the oil in a saucepan and gently fry the onion, celery and carrot until softened. Put in a liquidiser with the bulgar liquid and blend until smooth. Mix the blended vegetables with the buckwheat and bulgar and the remaining loaf ingredients.

Heat the oil for the filling and fry the onion until soft. Add the mushrooms and fry for another minute, then remove from the heat and mix in the remaining filling ingredients.

Spoon half of the loaf mixture into a base-lined and greased 8 inch / 20cm loaf tin. Press down firmly and evenly. Spread the filling on top, then the remaining loaf mixture, again pressing down evenly. Cover with foil and bake in a preheated oven at 180°C / 350°F / Gas mark 4 for 30 minutes. Remove the foil and bake for 10 minutes more. Run a sharp knife around the edges and invert the loaf onto a greased baking sheet. Peel off the lining and return to the oven for 10–15 minutes until golden. Cut into eight thick slices.

Crunchy sesame potato bake

2lb / 900g potatoes, peeled and diced

1 onion, peeled and finely chopped

2 garlic cloves, crushed

2 tablespoons sunflower oil

4 rounded tablespoons sesame seeds

black pepper

parsley

Boil the potatoes for 3 minutes, then drain. Heat the oil in a saucepan and gently fry the onion and garlic for 2 minutes. Add the diced potato and fry for a further 3 minutes. Remove from the heat and stir in the sesame seeds. Transfer the mixture to a shallow casserole dish, season with black pepper and sprinkle with parsley. Bake uncovered in a preheated oven at 190°C / 375°F / Gas mark 5 for 40–45 minutes until golden and crunchy.

Cauliflower in almond sauce

1lb / 450g cauliflower, cut into florets

1 onion, peeled and finely chopped

1 tablespoon vegetable oil

1oz / 25g ground almonds

1oz / 25g flaked almonds, toasted

8 fl.oz / 225ml water

8 fl.oz / 225ml soya milk

2 dessertspoons cornflour

1 teaspoon chervil

1/2 teaspoon yeast extract

black pepper

chopped fresh parsley

Heat the oil in a large saucepan and gently fry the onion until soft. Add the cauliflower, water and yeast extract, bring to the boil, cover and simmer until the cauliflower is just tender. Mix the ground almonds, cornflour and chervil with the soya milk and add to the pan. Season with black pepper and bring to the boil whilst stirring. Continue stirring until the sauce thickens. Add in half the flaked almonds and transfer to a warmed serving dish. Garnish with the remaining almonds and chopped fresh parsley.

Brussels sprouts with chestnuts

1¹/₄lb / 550g Brussels sprouts, peeled

8oz / 225g peeled frozen chestnuts, thawed

Cut a cross in the base of each Brussels sprout and steam with the chestnuts for approximately 10 minutes until just tender.

Cranberry and apple sauce

8oz / 225g fresh cranberries

12oz / 350g cooking apple, peeled, cored and grated

3oz / 75g light soft brown sugar

6 fl.oz / 175ml cider vinegar

Gently simmer the cranberries in the vinegar until they burst. Remove from the heat and stir in the sugar and apple. Return to the heat and simmer, stirring frequently, until the mixture thickens. Chill before serving.

Mincemeat, apple and almond charlottes

crumble mixture

3oz / 75g fresh wholemeal breadcrumbs

1oz / 25g ground almonds

1oz / 25g vegan margarine

$1/2$oz / 15g demerara sugar

$1/2$ teaspoon almond essence

fruit mixture

12oz / 350g cooking apple, peeled, cored and chopped

4oz / 100g mincemeat

2 fl.oz / 50ml fresh apple juice

topping

1 x 5oz / 150g pot of soya yoghurt

toasted flaked almonds

Gently heat the margarine with the almond essence until melted. Mix in the breadcrumbs, ground almonds and sugar, cook for a couple of minutes whilst stirring. Allow to cool then put in the fridge until cold. Cook the apple in the apple juice until just tender. Refrigerate until cold.

Assemble the charlottes an hour or two before serving. Mix the apple with the mincemeat and divide half of this mixture between four serving glasses. Spoon half the crumb mixture on top and press down lightly. Repeat these layers again and press down lightly. Cover and keep in the fridge until required. Top with the yoghurt and garnish with toasted flaked almonds just before serving.

FEBRUARY

You might celebrate:

Candlemas (February 2)

St Valentine's Day (February 14)

Washington's Birthday (USA: holiday date varies)

A Valentine's Day Feast

Pecan, wine and cranberry paté

•

Savoury fruity strudel

Parsley potatoes

Baked celeriac with ginger

Grated carrot and cardamon stir-fry

Mango and ginger relish

•

Malted mincemeat, coconut and oat slice

Pecan, wine and cranberry paté *Serves 6*

4oz / 100g pecans, grated

4oz / 100g celery, trimmed and finely chopped

2oz / 50g cranberry sauce

2oz / 50g millet

1oz / 25g fresh wholemeal breadcrumbs

1 onion, peeled and finely chopped

1 garlic clove, crushed

8 fl.oz / 225ml water

2 fl.oz / 50ml red wine

1 dessertspoon sunflower oil

1 teaspoon chervil

1/2 teaspoon paprika

1/2 teaspoon thyme

1/2 teaspoon yeast extract

black pepper

to serve

melba toast

salad garnish

Heat the oil in a saucepan and fry the celery, onion and garlic until soft. Add the millet, water and yeast extract and stir well, bring to the boil, cover and simmer until the liquid has been absorbed. Transfer the mixture to a blender, add the red wine and blend until smooth. Mix thoroughly with the remaining ingredients and spoon the mixture into a greased 6 inch / 15cm diameter ovenproof dish. Level the top and bake in a preheated oven at 180°C / 350°F / Gas mark 4 for about 45 minutes until set and golden. Serve cold with crusty wholemeal bread or melba toast and a salad garnish.

Savoury fruity strudel *Serves 6*

1 x 9¹/₂oz / 270g pack filo pastry

sunflower oil

sesame seeds

filling

8oz / 225g parsnip, peeled and grated

4oz / 100g peeled chestnuts, grated

4oz / 100g cooked black eye beans

2oz / 50g brazil nuts, grated

2oz / 50g mushrooms, wiped and finely chopped

1oz / 25g dried cranberries, chopped

1oz / 25g sultanas, chopped

¹/₂ oz / 15g soya flour

1 large Cox's apple, peeled, cored and finely chopped

1 onion, peeled and finely chopped

1 stick of celery, trimmed and finely chopped

4 tablespoons fresh fruit juice

1 tablespoon sunflower oil

1 teaspoon balsamic vinegar

1 teaspoon ground coriander

1 teaspoon ground cumin

¹/₄ teaspoon paprika

¹/₄ teaspoon ground cinnamon

black pepper

Heat the oil for the filling in a large saucepan and gently fry the parsnip, onion and celery for 3 minutes. Remove from the heat and mix in all the remaining ingredients except the fruit juice, soya flour and balsamic vinegar. Blend the soya flour with the fruit juice and vinegar until smooth, add to the mixture and stir well.

Brush a sheet of filo pastry with sunflower oil and put another sheet on top. Spread half the filling lengthwise along the centre of the sheet in an oblong measuring about 12 x 5 inches / 30 x 13cm. Repeat these layers and finish with two sheets of pastry, brushing between each with oil. Fold the two short sides in towards the centre, then do the same with the two longer sides. Carefully turn the strudel over onto a greased baking sheet. Brush the top with sunflower oil and sprinkle with sesame seeds. Cover with foil and bake in a preheated oven at 180°C / 350°F / Gas mark 4 for 20 minutes. Remove the foil and bake for a further 20–25 minutes until golden.

Parsley potatoes *Serves 6*

2¹/₄ lb / 1125g new potatoes, scraped

1 dessertspoon lemon juice

dressing

1 tablespoon olive oil

3 tablespoons white wine vinegar

3 rounded tablespoons finely chopped fresh parsley

black pepper

Cook the potatoes in a large pan of water with the lemon juice until tender. Mix the ingredients for the dressing. Drain the potatoes and return to the saucepan. Pour the dressing over the potatoes and toss around until they are coated. Transfer to a warmed serving dish.

Baked celeriac with ginger *Serves 6*

2¹/₄ lb / 1125g celeriac, peeled and chopped

¹/₂ oz / 15g root ginger, peeled and finely chopped

1 onion, peeled and finely chopped

1 tablespoon sunflower oil

6 fl.oz / 175ml soya milk

black pepper

chopped fresh chives

Heat the oil in a saucepan and fry the onion and ginger until soft. Add the celeriac and soya milk and season with black pepper. Simmer whilst stirring for 2 minutes. Transfer to a shallow casserole dish and cover tightly with foil. Bake in a preheated oven at 180°C / 350°F / Gas mark 4 for about 35 minutes until the celeriac is just tender. Serve garnished with chopped fresh chives.

Grated carrot and cardamom stir fry *Serves 6*

1½lb / 675g carrots, peeled and grated

4 cardamom pods, husked and the seeds separated

3 dessertspoons sunflower oil

black pepper

Heat the oil in a large frying pan or wok. Add the carrots and cardamom seeds and season with black pepper. Stir for a couple of minutes until the carrot is just tender.

Mango and ginger relish *Serves 6*

12oz / 350g mango flesh, chopped

³/₄ oz / 20g stem ginger, finely chopped

1 onion, peeled and finely chopped

4½ fl.oz / 137ml light malt vinegar

1½oz / 40g demerara sugar

½ teaspoon ground mace

Bring the onion and the vinegar to the boil, cover and simmer for 5 minutes. Remove from the heat and stir in the remaining ingredients. Return to the heat and simmer uncovered for about 15 minutes until the mixture is thick, stirring frequently to prevent sticking. Spoon into a serving bowl, cover and keep in the fridge until cold.

Malted mincemeat, coconut and oat slice *Serves 6*

8oz / 225g mincemeat

4oz / 100g porridge oats

4oz / 100g fine wholemeal self raising flour

3oz / 75g vegan margarine

2oz / 50g desiccated coconut

2 fl.oz / 50ml soya milk

1 rounded tablespoon malt extract

to serve

soya yoghurt or vegan ice cream

Melt the margarine and malt extract in a large saucepan. Remove from the heat and stir in the porridge oats, flour and coconut, add the soya milk and mix thoroughly. Spoon half the mixture into a greased 7 inch / 18cm diameter loose-bottomed deep flan tin, pressing it down firmly. Spread the mincemeat evenly on top, then the remaining mixture and again press down firmly. Bake in a preheated oven at 180°C / 350°F / Gas mark 4 for about 20 minutes until golden. Cut into wedges and serve hot with soya yoghurt or vegan ice cream.

MARCH

Drink a toast on

St David's Day (March 1)

St Patrick's Day (March 17)

Lady Day (March 25)

Mothering Sunday (4th Sunday in Lent)

Shrove Tuesday (Pancake Day)

Easter (this month maybe)

A Celtic Celebration

Pepperonata

•

Mushroom, courgette and cashew nut croustade

Paprika and onion sauce

Potato, leek and spinach casserole

Vegetable platter

Celery and apple relish

•

Apricot and hazelnut slice

Pepperonata *Serves 4/6*

1lb / 450g mixed peppers, sliced

12oz / 350g tomatoes, skinned and chopped

1 onion, peeled and sliced

2 garlic cloves, crushed

2 tablespoons olive oil

4 tablespoons water

1 teaspoon oregano

2 bay leaves

black pepper

chopped fresh parsley

to serve

crusty wholemeal French bread slices

Heat the oil and gently fry the mixed peppers, onion and garlic for 15 minutes. Add the remaining ingredients except the parsley and stir well. Cover and simmer for about 30 minutes until the peppers are tender and the mixture is thick, stirring frequently to prevent sticking. Put in a covered bowl in the fridge until cold. Spoon into little serving dishes and garnish with chopped fresh parsley. Serve with crusty wholemeal French bread slices.

Mushroom, courgette and cashew nut croustade

crumble

2oz / 50g cashew nuts, ground

2oz / 50g fresh wholemeal breadcrumbs

2oz / 50g medium oatmeal

2oz / 50g fine wholemeal self raising flour

2oz / 50g vegan margarine

1 tablespoon soya milk

filling

6oz / 175g mushrooms, wiped and finely chopped

6oz / 175g courgette, grated

2oz / 50g cashew nuts, ground

1 onion, peeled and finely chopped

1 garlic clove, crushed

1 dessertspoon sunflower oil

1/2 teaspoon thyme

1/2 teaspoon sage

black pepper

1 rounded tablespoon light tahini

Heat the oil for the filling and fry the onion and garlic until soft. Remove from the heat and mix in the remaining filling ingredients.

Melt the margarine in a saucepan. Remove from the heat and stir in the dry crumble ingredients. Add the milk and stir well. Spoon three-quarters of the mixture into a greased loose-bottomed 8 inch / 20cm diameter flan tin. Press down firmly and evenly. Spoon the filling over the base and distribute the remaining crumble evenly over the top, pressing lightly. Cover with foil and bake in a preheated oven at 180°C / 350°F / Gas mark 4 for 30 minutes. Remove the foil and bake for about 20 minutes more, until golden. Run a sharp knife around the edges and carefully remove the croustade from the tin.

Paprika and onion sauce

4oz / 100g onion, peeled and finely chopped

1 dessertspoon paprika

1 dessertspoon gravy powder

1 dessertspoon sunflower oil

1 teaspoon cornflour

1/2 teaspoon yeast extract

black pepper

5 fl.oz / 150ml soya milk

5 fl.oz / 150ml water

Heat the oil in a small saucepan and gently fry the onion until soft. Dissolve the paprika, gravy powder and cornflour in the soya milk and water and pour into a liquidiser. Add the onion and blend until smooth. Transfer to a clean pan, add the yeast extract and season with black pepper. Bring to the boil whilst stirring and continue stirring until the sauce thickens.

Potato, leek and spinach casserole

1lb / 450g potatoes, scraped

8oz / 225g leeks, trimmed and finely sliced

4oz / 100g frozen, cooked, chopped spinach, thawed

6 fl.oz / 175ml soya milk

black pepper

Cut the potatoes into $1/2$ inch / 1cm thick slices, then cut the slices into $1/2$ inch / 1cm wide chunks. Put the potatoes in a saucepan with the spinach and soya milk, stir well and bring to the boil. Simmer gently for 5 minutes, stirring frequently to prevent sticking. Remove from the heat and stir in the leeks, season with black pepper and mix well. Transfer to a casserole dish and cover tightly with foil. Bake in a preheated oven at 180°C / 350°F / Gas mark 4 for approximately 40 minutes until tender.

Vegetable platter

Choose a variety of vegetables and arrange them attractively on a platter garnished with chopped fresh herbs.

Per person:
Carrot: 4oz / 100g, cut into diagonal slices or sticks
Broccoli and cauliflower: 4–6oz / 100–175g, divided into florets
French beans: 4oz / 100g, just topped and tailed
Mangetout: 2-3oz / 50-75g, just topped and tailed
Miniature sweetcorn: 3oz / 75g, served whole
Swede: 4oz / 100g, cut into sticks
Courgette: 4oz / 100g, cut into diagonal slices

Celery and apple relish

8oz / 225g celery, trimmed and finely chopped
1 large red-skinned apple, cored and finely chopped
1 small onion, peeled and finely chopped
2oz / 50g raisins
1oz / 25g demerara sugar
5 fl.oz / 150ml white wine vinegar
1 teaspoon black mustard seeds
1/4 teaspoon ground mace
1/4 teaspoon ground allspice
1 teaspoon arrowroot
1 dessertspoon white wine vinegar

Put all the ingredients apart from the last two in a saucepan. Stir well and bring to the boil. Simmer uncovered for about 15 minutes until the liquid has been absorbed, stirring frequently to prevent sticking. Mix the arrowroot with the dessertspoonful of vinegar and add to the pan. Stir continuously whilst simmering for a couple of minutes until the mixture thickens. Transfer to a serving bowl, cover and chill before serving.

Apricot and hazelnut slice

pastry

5oz / 150g fine wholemeal self raising flour

1oz / 25g hazelnuts, ground

2oz / 50g vegan margarine

soya milk

filling

1 rounded tablespoon sugar-free apricot jam

1 x 14oz / 400g tin apricot halves in natural juice

4oz / 100g fine wholemeal self raising flour

1oz / 25g hazelnuts, ground

2oz / 50g vegan margarine

1oz / 25g demerara sugar

1 tablespoon apricot-flavoured liqueur

3 fl.oz / 75ml juice from tinned apricots

2 fl.oz / 50ml soya milk

1/2 oz / 15g hazelnuts, flaked

to serve

vegan ice cream or soya yoghurt

First make the pastry. Mix the flour with the ground hazelnuts and rub in the margarine. Add enough soya milk to bind then turn out onto a floured board. Knead well and roll out to fit a greased loose-bottomed 14 x 4 inch / 35 x 10cm flan tin. Prick the base and bake blind in a preheated oven at 170°C / 325F / Gas mark 3 for 5 minutes.

Cream the margarine with the sugar, then stir in the ground hazelnuts, soya milk and liqueur. Add the flour and juice and mix thoroughly until smooth. Spread the apricot jam evenly over the pastry base and spoon the sponge mixture on top. Pat the apricot halves dry on kitchen paper and cut each one in half. Press the apricot quarters into the sponge mixture lengthwise in a row along the centre of the flan. Sprinkle the flaked hazelnuts on top and return to the oven for approximately 25 minutes until golden brown. Cut into slices and serve either hot or cold with vegan ice cream or soya yoghurt.

APRIL

Festive dates:

Easter (probably)

St George's Day (April 23)

St George's Banquet

Marinated mushrooms

•

Pecan, vegetable and apple brioche

Avocado and potato purée

Orange-glazed swede julienne

Roast parsnips

Onion and sage sauce

•

Tropical fruit crumble

Marinated mushrooms

12oz / 350g button mushrooms, wiped and sliced

2 garlic cloves, crushed

2 spring onions, trimmed and finely chopped

1 tablespoon olive oil

3 fl.oz / 75ml white wine

2 teaspoons parsley

1 teaspoon soy sauce

black pepper

chopped fresh chives

to serve

melba toast

Heat the oil and gently fry the garlic and spring onions. Add the mushrooms and fry for another minute. Remove from the heat and add the white wine, parsley and soy sauce, season with black pepper and mix well. Put in a bowl, cover and keep in the fridge for at least six hours to allow the mushrooms to absorb the flavours. Transfer the mushrooms to little serving dishes and garnish with chopped fresh chives. Serve with melba toast.

Pecan, vegetable and apple brioche

pastry

8oz / 225g plain wholemeal flour

2oz / 50g vegan margarine

1 x ¼oz / 7g sachet easy-blend yeast

4 fl.oz / 125ml soya milk

extra soya milk

black onion seeds

filling

4oz / 100g pecans, grated

APRIL

Festive dates:

Easter (probably)

St George's Day (April 23)

St George's Banquet

Marinated mushrooms

•

Pecan, vegetable and apple brioche

Avocado and potato purée

Orange-glazed swede julienne

Roast parsnips

Onion and sage sauce

•

Tropical fruit crumble

Marinated mushrooms

12oz / 350g button mushrooms, wiped and sliced

2 garlic cloves, crushed

2 spring onions, trimmed and finely chopped

1 tablespoon olive oil

3 fl.oz / 75ml white wine

2 teaspoons parsley

1 teaspoon soy sauce

black pepper

chopped fresh chives

to serve

melba toast

Heat the oil and gently fry the garlic and spring onions. Add the mushrooms and fry for another minute. Remove from the heat and add the white wine, parsley and soy sauce, season with black pepper and mix well. Put in a bowl, cover and keep in the fridge for at least six hours to allow the mushrooms to absorb the flavours. Transfer the mushrooms to little serving dishes and garnish with chopped fresh chives. Serve with melba toast.

Pecan, vegetable and apple brioche

pastry

8oz / 225g plain wholemeal flour

2oz / 50g vegan margarine

1 x ¼oz / 7g sachet easy-blend yeast

4 fl.oz / 125ml soya milk

extra soya milk

black onion seeds

filling

4oz / 100g pecans, grated

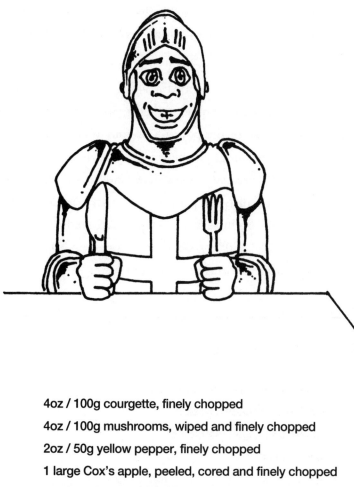

4oz / 100g courgette, finely chopped

4oz / 100g mushrooms, wiped and finely chopped

2oz / 50g yellow pepper, finely chopped

1 large Cox's apple, peeled, cored and finely chopped

1 onion, peeled and finely chopped

2 garlic cloves, crushed

1 rounded tablespoon soya flour

1 tablespoon vegetable oil

1 teaspoon chervil

1 teaspoon thyme

black pepper

Mix the flour and yeast in a bowl. Put the margarine and soya milk in a saucepan and heat until the margarine melts. Add to the flour and mix thoroughly until a soft dough forms. Knead well, then return to the bowl and cover. Leave in a warm place for 1 hour until doubled in size. Turn the dough out onto a floured board and knead again, then roll it out into an oblong shape measuring 12 x 9 inches / 30 x 23cm. Cover and leave for 30 minutes.

Heat the oil and gently fry the courgette, yellow pepper, onion and garlic for 4 minutes. Add the mushrooms and cook for a further minute. Remove from the heat and add the remaining filling ingredients. Spoon the mixture evenly lengthwise along the centre of the pastry. Carefully pull both sides of the pastry over to enclose the filling, pinching together where the sides meet. Transfer the brioche to a greased baking sheet and brush with soya milk. Using a sharp knife make a diagonal pattern on top, making sure not to cut right through the pastry. Sprinkle with black onion seeds and bake in a preheated oven at 180°C / 350°F / Gas mark 4 for about 30 minutes until golden. Cut the roll into four equal portions and serve.

Avocado and potato purée

> 1 large avocado, peeled and stoned
> 1¹/₂lb / 675g potatoes, peeled
> 1 tablespoon vegan margarine
> 1 teaspoon chives
> black pepper
> chopped fresh parsley

Boil the potatoes until done, then drain and dry off over a low heat. Chop the avocado and add to the potato together with the margarine and chives. Season with black pepper and mash the mixture until smooth and well combined. Spoon the pureé into a serving dish and cover with foil. Place in a preheated oven at 180°C / 350°F / Gas mark 4 for about 15 minutes until heated through. Garnish with chopped fresh parsley.

Orange-glazed swede julienne

1¹/₂lb / 675g swede, peeled and cut into julienne strips

8 fl.oz / 225ml fresh orange juice

1 tablespoon sunflower oil

1 teaspoon soy sauce

1 rounded teaspoon parsley

black pepper

Heat the oil in a large saucepan and gently fry the swede whilst stirring for 5 minutes. Dissolve the soy sauce in the orange juice and add to the pan together with the parsley. Season with black pepper and bring to the boil. Cover and simmer for 15-20 minutes until the juice has been absorbed and the swede is tender. Stir frequently to prevent sticking.

Roast parsnips

1¹/₂lb / 675g parsnips, peeled

vegetable oil

Cut the parsnips into even-sized chunks and boil for 2 minutes. Heat a little vegetable oil in a roasting tin in the oven, preheated at 200°C / 400°F / Gas mark 6. Drain the parsnips and put in the roasting tin. Spoon some of the hot oil over them and bake for about 35 minutes until golden, turning them occasionally to ensure even browning. Drain on kitchen paper before serving.

Onion and sage sauce

> 6oz / 175g onion, peeled and finely chopped
>
> ½oz / 15g vegan margarine
>
> ½oz / 15g cornflour
>
> 10 fl.oz / 300ml soya milk
>
> 2 teaspoons sage
>
> black pepper

Melt the margarine in a saucepan and gently fry the onion until soft. Dissolve the cornflour in the soya milk and add to the pan with the sage. Season with black pepper and bring to the boil whilst stirring. Contine stirring until the sauce thickens.

Tropical fruit crumble *Serves 6*

> **crumble**
>
> 2oz / 50g desiccated coconut
>
> 2oz / 50g porridge oats
>
> 2oz / 50g medium oatmeal
>
> 2oz / 50g vegan margarine
>
> 1oz / 25g fine wholemeal self raising flour
>
> 1oz / 25g flaked almonds
>
> 1 teaspoon ground cinnamon
>
> **filling**
>
> 1 x 8oz / 225g tin pineapple chunks in natural juice
>
> 4oz / 100g dessert dates, chopped
>
> 2 passion fruits
>
> 2 large bananas, peeled and sliced
>
> 1 large, just ripe mango, peeled and diced
>
> 3 tablespoons tropical fruit juice
>
> 2 tablespoons dark rum

1 tablespoon maple syrup

to serve

vegan ice cream or soya yoghurt

Strain the juice from the pineapple and put the pineapple chunks in a mixing bowl with the dates, banana and mango. Cut the passion fruits in half and scoop out the flesh. Add this to the other fruit with the tropical fruit juice, rum and maple syrup. Stir well, cover and leave for 30 minutes.

Melt the margarine over a low heat. Remove from the heat, stir in all the other crumble ingredients and mix thoroughly. Transfer the fruit to a shallow casserole dish and spread the crumble mixture evenly on top. Bake in a preheated oven at 170°C / 325°F / Gas mark 3 for about 25 minutes until golden. Serve hot with vegan ice cream or soya yoghurt.

MAY

Party pretexts:

Beltane / May Day (May 1)

May Day Bank Holiday

Spring Bank Holiday

Spring Frolic

---

*Smoky tofu and aubergine spread
with melba toast*

•

Leek, pineapple and pine kernel terrine

Potato and parsley oat balls

Carrot, ginger and orange purée

Cauliflower with savoury nut butter sauce

•

Raspberry and mandarin cups

Smoky tofu and aubergine spread with melba toast

spread
1lb / 450g aubergine
4oz / 100g smoked tofu
2oz / 50g smoked vegan 'cheddar', grated
olive oil
black pepper
1 teaspoon chives
melba toast
8 slices of medium-sliced wholemeal bread

Cut the aubergine in half lengthwise and make some slits in the flesh using a sharp knife. Brush the two halves all over with olive oil and bake in a preheated oven at 180°C / 350°F / Gas mark 4 for approximately 45 minutes until tender. Scoop the flesh out and put in a bowl. Allow the aubergine to cool, then add the remaining ingredients and either mash or blend until smooth. Transfer to a serving bowl and keep in the fridge until cold.

To make the melba toast, toast both sides of the bread, then trim off the crusts. Cut each slice into four triangles. Split each triangle in half horizontally to make 2 thin triangles. Place these untoasted side up under a hot grill until crisp. Leave to cool completely on a wire rack.

Leek, pineapple and pine kernel terrine

1lb / 450g leeks
filling
8oz / 225g tin pineapple chunks in natural juice
4oz / 100g pine kernels, grated
4oz / 100g long grain rice
4oz / 100g fresh wholemeal breadcrumbs
1 onion, peeled and finely chopped
1 tablespoon sunflower oil
1 teaspoon balsamic vinegar

1 teaspoon chervil

black pepper

water

Heat the oil in a large saucepan and fry the onion until softened. Add the rice and fry for another minute. Strain the juice from the tinned pineapple into a measuring jug, pressing out as much juice as possible from the chunks with the back of a spoon. Make the juice up to 12 fl.oz / 350ml with water and add to the pan together with the balsamic vinegar and chervil. Stir well and bring to the boil, cover and simmer until the liquid has been absorbed and the rice is cooked. Remove from the heat. Chop the pineapple chunks finely and add to the rice with the pine kernels and breadcrumbs. Season with black pepper and mix well.

Trim the leeks and discard the outer leaves. Cut them in half lengthwise and separate the leaves. Wash thoroughly, put in a large pan and cover with water. Bring to the boil, cover and simmer for 3 minutes, then drain.

Line an 8 inch / 20cm loaf tin with greased foil. Use the blanched leek leaves to line the tin by overlapping each leaf, leaving an overhang around each side for folding over the filling. Spoon the filling into the lined tin and press down firmly and evenly. Fold the overhanging leaves over the filling to enclose it completely. Cover loosely with foil and bake in a preheated oven at 180°C / 350°F / Gas mark 4 for 40 minutes. Carefully invert onto a serving plate and cut into slices with a sharp knife.

Potato and parsley oat balls

1lb / 450g potatoes, scraped and diced

2oz / 50g vegan 'cheddar', grated

2oz / 50g porridge oats

1oz / 25g fresh parsley, finely chopped

1oz / 25g vegan margarine

black pepper

oatbran

Boil the potatoes, drain and dry off over a low heat. Mash with the margarine, then stir in the 'cheddar', parsley and porridge oats. Season with black pepper and mix thoroughly. Take rounded dessertspoonfuls of the mixture and shape into balls. Roll each ball in oatbran until completely covered and put on a greased baking sheet. Bake in a preheated oven at 180°C / 350°F / Gas mark 4 for 30 minutes until golden.

Carrot, ginger and orange purée

1¹/₂lb / 675g carrots, scraped and chopped

6 fl.oz / 175ml fresh orange juice

¹/₂oz / 15g fresh root ginger, peeled and finely chopped

1 dessertspoon sunflower oil

¹/₄ teaspoon yeast extract

¹/₂ teaspoon ground coriander

black pepper

Heat the oil in a saucepan and gently fry the root ginger until soft. Add the remaining ingredients and stir well. Bring to the boil, cover and simmer for 10-15 minutes until the carrots are tender. Blend until smooth. Spoon into a serving dish, cover with foil and place in a preheated oven at 180°C / 350°F / Gas mark 4 for about 15 minutes until heated through.

Cauliflower with savoury nut butter sauce

1lb / 450g cauliflower, cut into florets

sauce

1 rounded tablespoon smooth nut butter (peanut, cashew, hazelnut or mixed nut)

1 rounded dessertspoon cornflour

¹/₂ teaspoon yeast extract

black pepper

10 fl / oz / 300ml soya milk

Steam the cauliflower until just tender. Meanwhile, make the sauce. Mix the cornflour with the soya milk until smooth, pour into a small saucepan and add the remaining ingredients. Bring to the boil whilst stirring and continue stirring for a minute or two until the sauce thickens. Transfer the cooked cauliflower to a warmed serving dish and pour the sauce over it.

Raspberry and mandarin cups *Serves 6*

2 x 10oz / 300g tins mandarins in natural juice

8oz / 225g raspberries (if frozen, thaw first)

1 tablespoon demerara sugar

1 teaspoon agar agar

2 x 5oz / 150g pots raspberry-flavoured soya yoghurt

Strain the juice from the mandarins into a liquidiser. Divide the mandarin segments between six serving glasses. Keep 6 raspberries for garnish and put the remainder in the liquidiser. Liquidise the raspberries with the mandarin juice until smooth. Strain the purée into a saucepan and discard the pips. Add the sugar and agar agar and stir until dissolved. Heat gently whilst stirring until just below boiling point, then pour over the mandarins in the glasses. Cover and chill for a couple of hours until set. Top each dessert with yoghurt and garnish with a raspberry.

JUNE

Why not celebrate:

Summer solstice (June 21)

Midsummer Day (24)

Father's Day

Midsummer Fare

Raddichio leaves with spiced quinoa salad

•

Aubergine, almond and lentil paté en croûte

Apple sauce

Potato and spinach purée

Asparagus gratin

•

Rum and raisin exotic fruit savarin

Raddichio leaves with spiced quinoa salad *Serves 6*

6 raddichio leaves

4oz / 100g quinoa

2oz / 50g dessert dates, stoned and finely chopped

2oz / 50g dried apricots, cooked and finely chopped

2oz / 50g red pepper, finely chopped

1oz / 25g sultanas

1oz / 25g pumpkin seeds

8 fl.oz / 225ml water

1 rounded teaspoon curry paste

3 cardamoms, husked and the seeds separated

Put the quinoa, water and curry paste in a saucepan and stir well. Bring to the boil, cover and simmer for about 10 minutes until the liquid has been

absorbed, stirring frequently to prevent sticking. Transfer to a bowl, cover and put in the fridge until cold.

Mix the dates with the apricots, red pepper, sultanas, pumpkin and cardamom seeds. Add to the cold quinoa and mix thoroughly. Divide this mixture between the raddichio leaves.

Aubergine, almond and lentil paté en croûte
Serves 6

pastry
8oz / 225g fine wholemeal self raising flour

2¹/₂oz / 65g vegan margarine

1 rounded tablespoon almond butter

soya milk

filling
12oz / 350g aubergine, finely chopped

4oz / 100g ground almonds

4oz / 100g puy lentils

4oz / 100g dessert dates, stoned and finely chopped

1oz / 25g fresh wholemeal breadcrumbs

1 onion, peeled and finely chopped

2 garlic cloves, crushed

2 tablespoons sunflower oil

1 teaspoon paprika

1 teaspoon ground coriander

black pepper

Cook the lentils until done, then drain in a fine sieve and press out excess water with the back of a spoon. Mash the lentils and set aside. Heat the oil in a large saucepan and gently fry the aubergine, onion and garlic for about 15 minutes until soft. Stir frequently to prevent sticking. Remove from the heat, add the mashed lentils and remaining filling ingredients and mix thoroughly.

Rub the margarine and almond butter into the flour. Add enough soya milk to bind, turn onto a floured surface and knead. Take half the dough and roll it out to fit the base of a lined and greased 9 x 7 inch / 23 x 18cm baking tin or casserole dish. Spread the filling evenly over the dough and press down firmly. Roll out the other piece of dough to fit over the top. Press this down lightly and brush with soya milk. Using a sharp knife score diagonal lines on top to make a diamond pattern. Cover with foil and bake in a preheated oven at 180°C / 350°F / Gas mark 4 for 25 minutes. Remove the foil and bake for about 15 minutes more until golden.

Apple sauce *Serves 6*

1¹/₄lb / 550g cooking apple, peeled, cored and chopped

2 tablespoons fresh apple juice

1 rounded dessertspoon demerara sugar

squeeze of fresh lemon juice

12 cloves

Put all ingredients in a saucepan and simmer gently until the apple is soft. Take off the heat and remove the cloves. Mash the apple until smooth. Transfer to a serving bowl, cover and refrigerate before serving.

Potato and spinach purée *Serves 6*

2¹/₄lb / 1kg potatoes, peeled and chopped

4oz / 100g frozen, cooked, chopped spinach, thawed

3 fl.oz / 75ml soya milk

1 rounded tablespoon vegan margarine

pinch of grated nutmeg

black pepper

Boil the potatoes, drain and dry off over a low heat. Add the spinach, margarine and nutmeg and mash until smooth. Stir in the soya milk and season with black pepper. Mix thoroughly, then spoon into a serving dish. Cover with foil and place in a preheated oven at 180°C / 350°F / Gas mark 4 for about 15 minutes until heated through.

Asparagus gratin *Serves 6*

1¹/₂lb / 675g thin asparagus

sauce

1lb 2oz / 500g tomatoes, skinned and chopped

6oz / 175g fennel bulb, finely chopped

1 large onion, peeled and finely chopped

6 garlic cloves, crushed

6 tablespoons white wine

2 tablespoons olive oil

2 tablespoons tomato purée

1 rounded teaspoon oregano

1 teaspoon basil

1 teaspoon thyme

black pepper

topping

1¹/₂oz / 40g fresh wholemeal breadcrumbs

1¹/₂oz / 40g vegan 'cheddar', grated

1 rounded tablespoon vegan 'parmesan' substitute

1 rounded teaspoon parsley

Trim any woody parts from the asparagus and cut the stalks in half. Steam the asparagus until just tender (the asparagus tips will require less cooking than the bottom part of the stalks). Arrange the asparagus in a casserole dish.

Heat the oil and fry the onion, fennel and garlic until soft. Add the tomatoes and remaining sauce ingredients and stir well. Bring to the boil, cover and simmer for 2 minutes. Spoon the sauce over the asparagus.

Mix the topping ingredients and spread evenly over the sauce. Cover the dish with foil and bake in a preheated oven at 180°C / 350°F / Gas mark 4 for 20 minutes. Remove the foil and bake for a further 5 minutes until golden.

Rum and raisin exotic fruit savarin *Serves 6*

savarin

6oz / 175g fine wholemeal self raising flour

2oz / 50g raisins, finely chopped

2oz / 50g vegan margarine

1oz / 25g demerara sugar

half a ¼oz / 7g sachet easy-blend yeast

10 fl.oz / 300ml soya milk

syrup

1 rounded dessertspoon golden syrup

2 tablespoons dark rum

4 tablespoons fresh fruit juice

filling

selection of prepared exotic fruits (star fruit, mango, paw paw etc.)

Mix the flour, raisins, soya flour, sugar and yeast in a bowl. Put the margarine and soya milk in a saucepan and heat gently until the margarine melts. Add to the mixing bowl and mix together well. Spoon the mixture evenly into a greased 8 inch / 20cm diameter ring mould. Cover and leave to stand in a warm place for 1 hour until well risen. Uncover and bake in a preheated oven at 180°C / 350°F / Gas mark 4 for about 20 minutes until golden. Run a sharp knife around the edges to loosen, then invert onto a wire rack and allow to cool.

Heat the golden syrup with the rum and fruit juice until it dissolves. Put a plate under the savarin on the wire rack to catch the syrup and pour the hot syrup over the savarin until it soaks in. Transfer to a serving plate, cover and chill for a couple of hours. Spoon the exotic fruit mixture into the centre and serve.

JULY

Have a party on:

Independence Day (USA: July 4)

St Swithin's Feast Day (July 15)

Alfresco Buffet

Mushroom and olive dip with crudités

•

Herby rice and vegetable ring

Chick pea and tofu croquettes with
cucumber and gherkin salsa

Tartare potato salad

Beansprout, peanut and mango salad

•

Strawberry and orange sundaes

Mushroom and olive dip with crudités

dip

12oz / 350g mushrooms, wiped and chopped

1 onion, peeled and chopped

1 garlic clove, crushed

12 green olives, chopped

1 tablespoon olive oil

1 dessertspoon balsamic vinegar

1 teaspoon thyme

1 teaspoon parsley

black pepper

5 fl.oz / 150ml water

Heat the oil and gently fry the onion and garlic until soft. Add the mushrooms and fry for 2 minutes more. Remove from the heat and allow to cool slightly. Transfer to a blender and add the remaining ingredients. Blend until smooth, then pour into a serving bowl. Cover and chill before serving.

crudités

Allow 12oz–1lb / 350–450g of fresh vegetables for four servings. To prepare the crudités, simply wash, scrape or peel the vegetables and cut them into strips or even-sized chunks. Arrange on a serving plate around the bowl containing the dip.

Herby rice and vegetable ring

8oz / 225g long grain brown rice

4oz / 100g carrot, scraped and grated

2oz / 50g green pepper, finely chopped

2oz / 50g red pepper, finely chopped

2oz / 50g vegan 'cheddar', grated

1 onion, peeled and grated

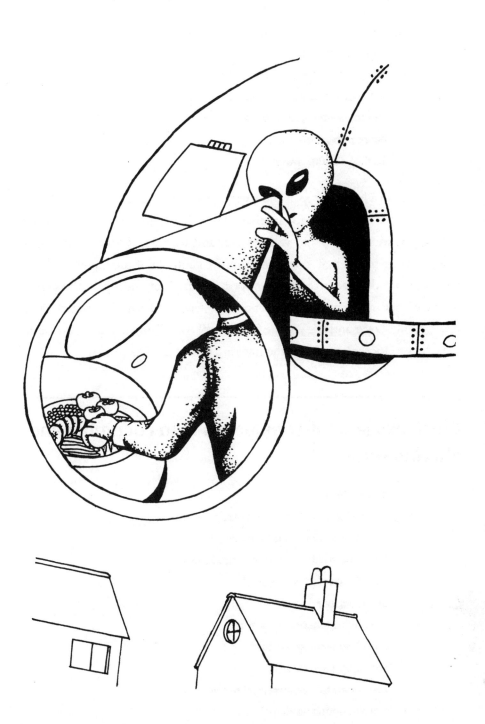

2 garlic cloves, crushed

1 tablespoon olive oil

1 rounded teaspoon dried mint

1 rounded teaspoon marjoram

1/4 teaspoon yeast extract

black pepper

18 fl.oz / 550ml water

Heat the oil in a large saucepan and fry the onion and garlic until soft. Add the rice and cook whilst stirring for another 2 minutes. Stir in the carrot, green and red pepper, mint, marjoram, yeast extract and water, and season with black pepper. Bring to the boil, cover and simmer gently until the liquid has been absorbed and the rice is ready. Remove from the heat and stir in the grated 'cheddar'. Spoon the mixture into an oiled 7^1/2inch / 19cm ring mould. Press down evenly, cover and keep in the fridge until cold. Run a sharp knife around the edges to loosen and invert the rice ring onto a serving plate.

Chick pea and tofu croquettes with cucumber and gherkin salsa

croquettes

8oz / 225g cooked chick peas, mashed

8oz / 225g smoked tofu, mashed

2oz / 50g fresh wholemeal breadcrumbs

1 onion, peeled and grated

black pepper

1 rounded teaspoon chervil

1oz / 25g wholemeal flour

1oz / 25g soya flour

1 rounded tablespoon light tahini

5 tablespoons soya milk

1/2 teaspoon yeast extract

sesame seeds

Put the mashed chick peas and tofu in a mixing bowl and add the bread-crumbs, onion, chervil and wholemeal flour. Stir well. Blend the soya flour with the tahini, soya milk and yeast extract until smooth. Add to the chick pea mixture and season with black pepper. Mix thoroughly until well combined. Take rounded tablespoonfuls of the mixture and shape into croquettes. Roll these in sesame seeds until completely covered and put them on a greased baking sheet. Bake in a preheated oven at 180°C / 350°F / Gas mark 4 for 30 minutes until golden brown. Allow the croquettes to cool, then keep in the fridge until cold.

salsa
6oz / 175g cucumber, finely chopped
2oz / 50g gherkins, finely chopped
1 tablespoon white wine vinegar
1 dessertspoon olive oil
1 teaspoon pesto
black pepper
cucumber slices

Put the chopped cucumber and gherkins in a mixing bowl. Mix the pesto with the olive oil and vinegar and pour over the cucumber and gherkins. Season with black pepper and toss well.

Arrange some cucumber slices around the edge of a serving dish and pile the salsa in the centre. Cover and chill for a couple of hours. Put the dish on a large plate and arrange the croquettes around it.

Tartare potato salad

1¹/₂lb / 675g new potatoes, scraped

2 rounded tablespoons vegan tartare sauce

2 tablespoons white wine vinegar

2 gherkins, finely chopped

2 spring onions, trimmed and finely chopped

chopped fresh chives

Boil the potatoes until just done, drain and rinse under cold running water. Dice the potatoes and put them in a mixing bowl with the gherkins and spring onions. Mix the tartare sauce with the vinegar until smooth and spoon this over the potato mixture. Toss thoroughly and transfer the salad to a serving bowl. Garnish with chopped fresh chives and chill before serving.

Beansprout, peanut and mango salad

8oz / 225g beansprouts

3oz / 75g cucumber, diced

1oz / 25g roasted peanuts, toasted

1 small mango, peeled and diced

2 spring onions, trimmed and finely sliced

shredded Chinese leaves

dressing

1 rounded dessertspoon peanut butter

1 dessertspoon sunflower oil

¹/₂ teaspoon soy sauce

Put the beansprouts, cucumber, peanuts, mango and spring onions in a bowl. Mix the dressing ingredients together until smooth and pour over the salad. Toss well. Arrange some shredded Chinese leaves on a serving plate and spoon the salad on top. Cover and chill.

Strawberry and orange sundaes

8oz / 225g strawberries

6oz / 175g vegan 'cream cheese'

5 fl.oz / 150ml fresh orange juice

1 teaspoon agar agar

1 large orange

2 tablespoons Cointreau

Blend 6oz / 175g of the strawberries with the 'cream cheese' until smooth. Dissolve the agar agar in the orange juice and heat until just below boiling point. Add to the strawberry purée and mix well. Keep 4 strawberries for garnish and chop the rest. Peel the orange and remove all the pith and membranes. Chop the segments, mix with the chopped strawberries and divide between four serving glasses. Sprinkle with the Cointreau. Spoon the strawberry purée over the fruit and top with a whole strawberry. Cover and keep in the fridge for a few hours until cold and set.

AUGUST

Excuses for a party:

Lammas (August 1)

Summer Bank Holiday

Holiday Spread

Asparagus and mushroom soup

•

Chick pea, cashew nut and cranberry pie

Savoury apple and potato bake

Broccoli with carrot, orange and tahini sauce

Salad platter

•

Tropical fruit platter with apricot and
vanilla cream and paradise mix

Asparagus and mushroom soup

12oz / 350g asparagus

4oz / 100g mushrooms, wiped and sliced

1 onion, peeled and chopped

1 tablespoon sherry

1 dessertspoon vegetable oil

1 teaspoon parsley

1/4 teaspoon yeast extract

black pepper

25 fl.oz / 750ml water or light vegetable stock

3 fl.oz / 75ml soya milk

Remove any woody parts from the asparagus. Heat the oil in a large saucepan and fry the onion until softened. Stir in the chopped asparagus and mushrooms and fry for another minute. Add all remaining ingredients except the soya milk, and stir well. Bring to the boil, cover and simmer for about 15 minutes until the asparagus is tender. Remove from the heat and allow to cool slightly, then liquidise until smooth. Pour through a fine sieve into the cleaned pan. Add the soya milk, stir well and reheat whilst stirring.

Chick pea, cashew nut and cranberry pie

9oz / 250g puff pastry

filling

6oz / 175g cooked chick peas, grated

4oz / 100g cashew nuts, grated

4oz / 100g carrot, scraped and grated

2oz / 50g cranberry sauce

1oz / 25g dried cranberries, chopped

2 celery sticks, trimmed and finely chopped

1 onion, peeled and finely chopped

2 garlic cloves, crushed

1 tablespoon sunflower oil

1 teaspoon soy sauce

1 teaspoon parsley

1 teaspoon chives

1 teaspoon paprika

black pepper

soya milk

sesame seeds

Heat the oil in a large saucepan and fry the onion, celery and garlic until softened. Remove from the heat and add all remaining ingredients except the soya milk and sesame seeds. Mix thoroughly and set aside.

Take three-quarters of the pastry and roll it out on a floured board to fit a lined and greased 8 inch / 20cm diameter flan tin. Spoon the filling evenly into the pastry case. Roll out the remaining pastry to an 8 inch / 20cm circle and place on top. Press the edges of the pastry together with a fork. Score a diagonal pattern on the top with a sharp knife, prick all over with a fork and brush with soya milk. Sprinkle with sesame seeds and bake in a preheated oven at 170°C / 325F / Gas mark 3 for 35–40 minutes until golden brown.

Savoury apple and potato bake

1lb / 450g new potatoes, scraped and sliced

1lb / 450g apples, peeled, cored and thickly sliced

8oz / 225g leek, trimmed and finely chopped

2oz / 50g vegan 'cheddar', grated

10 fl.oz / 300ml soya milk

1/2oz / 15g cornflour

1 tablespoon vegetable oil

2 teaspoons parsley

1/2 teaspoon grated nutmeg

black pepper

chives

Boil the potato slices for 3 minutes, then drain and set aside. Heat the oil in a saucepan and fry the leek until soft. Dissolve the cornflour in the milk and add together with the parsley, nutmeg and half of the grated 'cheddar'. Season with black pepper and bring to the boil whilst stirring. Continue stirring until the sauce thickens. Remove from the heat and add the potato and apple slices. Transfer to a casserole dish and spread the remaining grated 'cheddar' on top. Sprinkle with chives and cover with foil. Bake in a preheated oven at 180°C / 350°F / Gas mark 4 for about 30 minutes until the potato is cooked.

Broccoli with carrot, orange and tahini sauce

1lb / 450g broccoli, cut into florets

sauce

4oz / 100g carrot, scraped and grated

1 dessertspoon sunflower oil

1 dessertspoon light tahini

1 teaspoon soy sauce

1 dessertspoon cornflour

4 fl.oz / 125ml fresh orange juice

4 fl.oz / 125ml water

1/4 teaspoon caraway seeds, crushed

black pepper

Steam the broccoli until just tender. Meanwhile, make the sauce. Heat the oil in a small saucepan and gently fry the carrot until softened. Mix the tahini, soy sauce, orange juice, water and cornflour until smooth. Add to the pan with the crushed caraway seeds and season with black pepper. Stir whilst bringing to the boil and continue stirring until the sauce thickens. Put the broccoli in a warmed serving dish and spoon the sauce over it.

Salad platter

Make up a platter of seasonal salad vegetables, arranged attractively in a circle. Start from the outside and work towards the centre. Garnish the platter with fresh herbs and chopped nuts.

Tropical fruit platter with apricot and vanilla cream and paradise mix *Serves 6*

1¹/₂lb / 675g prepared tropical fruits (paw paw, mango, pineapple, lychee, melon, star fruit etc.)

apricot and vanilla cream

4oz / 100g dried apricots

5 fl.oz / 150ml fresh orange juice

2 x 125g pots vegan vanilla-flavoured dessert

paradise mix

4oz / 100g dried papaya

4oz / 100g dried pineapple

2oz / 50g dried dates

2oz / 50g cashew nuts

2oz / 50g brazil nuts

2oz / 50g toasted flaked coconut

Prepare the apricot and vanilla cream first. Soak the apricots in water for 2 hours, then drain and chop finely. Put them in a saucepan with the orange juice and bring to the boil. Cover and simmer gently until the juice has been absorbed and the apricots are soft. Refrigerate until cold. When cold blend the apricots with the vanilla-flavoured dessert until smooth and put back in the fridge until required.

Chop all ingredients for the paradise mix and stir well. Store in an airtight container until required.

Arrange the prepared tropical fruits on a serving platter or large plate and serve the cream and the paradise mix in separate bowls alongside.

SEPTEMBER

Make merry at

Michaelmas (September 29)

Harvest Supper

Stuffed avocado pears

•

Tempeh and mixed nut plait

Boiled potatoes with garlic and parsley sauce

Courgette provençale

Wheaty corn and bean salad

Fresh tomato and gherkin relish

•

*Marinated liqueur fruits with melon balls
and ice cream*

Stuffed avocado pears

2 small avocado pears

6oz / 175g cooked chick peas, grated

2oz / 50g vegan 'cream cheese'

2 teaspoons lemon juice

2 teaspoons chives

black pepper

4 fresh parsley sprigs

Cut the avocado pears in half and remove the stones. Scoop out the flesh with a spoon and mash it together with the lemon juice. Add the chick peas, vegan 'cream cheese' and chives, and season with black pepper. Mix thoroughly, spoon the mixture back into the avocado shells and fork over the tops. Chill for 1 hour. Garnish each half with a sprig of fresh parsley before serving.

Tempeh and mixed nut plait

9oz / 250g puff pastry

filling

8oz / 225g tempeh, grated

4oz / 100g carrot, scraped and grated

2oz / 50g mixed nuts, grated

2oz / 50g fresh wholemeal breadcrumbs

1 onion, peeled and finely chopped

1 garlic clove, crushed

6 tablespoons water

1 rounded tablespoon mixed nut butter

1 dessertspoon vegetable oil

1 teaspoon soy sauce

1 teaspoon parsley

black pepper

soya milk

poppy seeds

Heat the oil in a large saucepan and fry the onion and garlic until soft. Remove from the heat and add the tempeh, carrot, mixed nuts, breadcrumbs and parsley. Mix the nut butter with the water and soy sauce until smooth and add to the tempeh mixture. Season with black pepper and combine thoroughly.

Roll out the pastry to an oblong shape of 14 x 10 inches / 35 x 25cm. Spoon the filling evenly along the middle of the pastry lengthwise. Cut horizontal strips 3/4inch / 2cm wide to within 1/2inch / 1cm of the filling on the long sides of the pastry. Lift alternate strips of pastry over the filling to enclose it completely and give a plaited effect. Brush with soya milk and sprinkle with poppy seeds. Bake in a preheated oven at 170°C / 325°F / Gas mark 3 for about 35 minutes until golden brown.

Boiled potatoes with garlic and parsley sauce

2lb / 900g small even-sized potatoes, scraped

sauce

2 garlic cloves, crushed

1/2oz / 15g vegan margarine

1/2oz / 15g cornflour

10 fl.oz / 300ml soya milk

2 dessertspoons parsley

black pepper

Boil the potatoes while making the sauce. Melt the margarine in a saucepan and gently fry the garlic for a couple of minutes. Add the cornflour and mix well, then stir in the soya milk. Transfer to a liquidiser and blend until smooth. Return to the saucepan, add the parsley and season with black pepper. Bring to the boil whilst stirring and continue stirring until the sauce thickens. Drain the potatoes and place in a warmed serving dish. Pour the sauce over the potatoes and serve.

Courgette provençale

1lb / 450g courgettes, sliced

12oz / 350g tomatoes, skinned and chopped

1 onion, peeled and finely chopped

2 garlic cloves, crushed

1 tablespoon olive oil

1 dessertspoon tomato purée

1 teaspoon parsley

1 teaspoon basil

black pepper

finely chopped fresh mixed herbs

Heat the oil in a saucepan and fry the onion and garlic until soft. Add the tomatoes, tomato purée, parsley and basil and season with black pepper. Bring to the boil and simmer gently until the tomatoes become pulpy.

Meanwhile, steam the courgette slices until just tender. Add the courgette to the sauce, stir well and continue cooking for 1 minute. Transfer to a warmed serving dish and garnish with the chopped fresh herbs.

Wheaty corn and bean salad

8oz / 225g sweetcorn kernels

4oz / 100g wheat berries

4oz / 100g cooked black eye beans

2oz / 50g raisins

2 spring onions, trimmed and finely sliced

2 cocktail gherkins, finely chopped

2 dessertspoons white wine vinegar

2 teaspoons sunflower oil

1 teaspoon soy sauce

black pepper

Soak the wheat berries in water overnight. Rinse and put them in a fresh pan of water. Bring to the boil, cover and simmer for about 45 minutes until tender. Drain and transfer to a mixing bowl. Blanch the sweetcorn kernels, drain and add to the wheat berries together with the black eye beans, raisins, onions and gherkins. Mix the vinegar with the sunflower oil and soy sauce and pour over the salad. Season with black pepper and toss well. Transfer to a serving bowl, cover and chill before serving.

Fresh tomato and gherkin relish

12oz / 350g firm ripe tomatoes, skinned and chopped

4 cocktail gherkins, finely chopped

1 dessertspoon olive oil

1 dessertspoon white wine vinegar

1 teaspoon parsley

$^1/_2$ teaspoon basil

black pepper

Put the tomatoes in a bowl and add the gherkins, parsley and basil. Mix the olive oil with the vinegar and add. Season with black pepper and mix thoroughly. Put in a serving bowl, cover and chill.

Marinated liqueur fruits with melon balls and ice cream

1 medium-sized ripe melon

vegan ice cream

marinated liqueur fruits

4oz / 100g dried apricots, finely chopped

4oz / 100g dried dates, finely chopped

4oz / 100g glacé cherries, washed, dried and chopped

4oz / 100g raisins

4oz / 100g sultanas

4 fl.oz / 125ml fruit-flavoured liqueur

2 fl.oz / 50ml brandy

Put all ingredients for the marinated liqueur fruits in a bowl and stir well. Cover and keep in the fridge for 48 hours, stirring a few times to ensure even absorption of the liquid.

Cut the melon in half and remove the seeds and pith. Form the flesh into balls using a melon baller. Refrigerate the melon balls for a couple of hours until cold. Serve with the liqueur fruits and top with vegan ice cream.

OCTOBER

Reasons to party:

St Francis' Feast Day (October 4)

Hallowe'en (October 30)

Hallowe'en Party

Sparkling melon soup

•

Festive layered pie

Sweet potato with coconut

Cranberry-glazed cabbage

Bread sauce

Red onion relish

•

Truffle pudding

Sparkling melon soup

1 large Galia melon

5 fl.oz / 150ml fresh apple juice

4 fl.oz / 125ml sparkling white wine

4 fresh mint leaves

Cut the melon in half and make 12 balls using a melon baller. Keep these for garnish. Remove the pips and peel from the melon and chop the flesh. Blend the melon in a liquidiser with the apple juice and wine until smooth, then put in the fridge for a few hours until cold. Divide the soup between four bowls and garnish each with 3 melon balls and a fresh mint leaf.

Festive layered pie   *Serves 6*

pastry

12oz / 350g fine wholemeal self raising flour

4oz / 100g vegan margarine

4 fl.oz / 125ml soya milk

1 teaspoon paprika

extra soya milk

sesame seeds

layer 1

1lb / 450g pumpkin flesh, diced

8oz / 225g potato, peeled and chopped

1 dessertspoon vegan margarine

$1/4$ teaspoon ground mace

black pepper

layer 2

4oz / 100g mushrooms, wiped and finely chopped

4oz / 100g shelled chestnuts, grated

2oz / 50g dried dates, finely chopped

1oz / 25g walnuts, grated

1 onion, peeled and finely chopped

1 tablespoon vegetable oil

pinch of grated nutmeg

1 teaspoon soy sauce

black pepper

layer 3

8oz / 225g Brussels sprouts, peeled

4oz / 100g leek, trimmed and finely chopped

1oz / 25g vegan 'cheddar', grated

1oz / 25g pistachio nuts, grated

1 celery stick, trimmed and finely sliced

1 dessertspoon vegetable oil

1 teaspoon chervil

1 teaspoon parsley

black pepper

First make layer 1. Steam the pumpkin until tender, then mash until smooth. Boil the potato until done, then drain and dry off over a low heat. Mash with the margarine and add to the pumpkin, together with the ground mace. Season with black pepper, mix thoroughly and set aside.

Heat the oil for layer 2 in a saucepan and fry the onion until soft. Add the mushrooms and fry until the juices run, then the chestnuts and stir around for 1 minute. Remove from the heat and add the walnuts, dates, nutmeg and soy sauce. Season with black pepper, mix thoroughly and set aside.

For layer 3, steam the sprouts until just done, then chop them finely. Heat the oil in a saucepan and fry the leek and celery until soft. Remove from the heat and add the chopped sprouts, grated 'cheddar', pistachios, chervil and parsley. Season with black pepper and mix well.

Allow all the layers to cool whilst making the pastry. Sift the flour and paprika into a mixing bowl. Melt the margarine in the soya milk. Add to the flour and mix thoroughly until a soft dough forms. Knead well. Roll out three-quarters of the dough on a floured board to line a greased 7 inch / 18cm diameter loose-bottomed cake tin. Spoon layer 1 into the pastry case, pressing down firmly and evenly, then layers 2 and 3.

Roll out the remaining pastry to a 7 inch / 18cm circle and place on top. Press the edges of the pastry together with a fork and prick the top all over. Brush with soya milk and sprinkle with sesame seeds. Cover with foil and bake in a preheated oven at 180°C / 350°F / Gas mark 4 for 40 minutes. Remove the foil and bake for a further 10–15 minutes until golden brown. Run a sharp knife around the edge and carefully remove the pie from the tin. Cut into wedges to serve.

Sweet potato with coconut

> 1¹/₂lb / 675g sweet potato, peeled and diced
>
> 1 onion, peeled and finely chopped
>
> 2 tablespoons vegetable oil
>
> 2 tablespoons water
>
> 1 rounded tablespoon desiccated coconut
>
> 1 teaspoon yellow mustard seeds
>
> 1 teaspoon cumin seeds
>
> 1 teaspoon turmeric
>
> garam masala

Boil the potatoes until just cooked, drain and set aside. Heat the oil in a saucepan and gently fry the onion until soft. Add the coconut, mustard seeds, cumin seeds and turmeric and stir around for 2 minutes. Add the potato and water and stir well. Cook gently whilst stirring for a few minutes until heated through. Put into a warmed serving dish and sprinkle lightly with garam masala.

Cranberry-glazed cabbage

1lb / 450g red cabbage, trimmed and shredded

3 rounded tablespoons cranberry sauce

2 tablespoons cranberry or apple juice

1 teaspoon black mustard seeds

Steam the cabbage until just tender. Put the cranberry sauce, juice and mustard seeds in a large saucepan and stir whilst heating gently. Add the steamed cabbage and stir over a low heat for a couple of minutes until well combined. Transfer to a warmed serving dish.

Bread sauce

2oz / 50g fresh wholemeal breadcrumbs

1 onion, peeled and sliced

12 fl.oz / 350ml soya milk

$^1/_2$oz / 15g vegan margarine

$^1/_2$ teaspoon allspice berries

$^1/_2$ teaspoon cloves

black pepper

1 tablespoon vegan 'cream'

Put the onion, allspice berries and cloves in a saucepan with the soya milk. Bring to the boil, cover and simmer for 5 minutes. Strain the soya milk into another saucepan and add the margarine. Heat whilst stirring until the margarine melts. Remove from the heat and mix in the breadcrumbs and 'cream'. Season with black pepper and leave for 20 minutes. Transfer to a double boiler and heat gently before serving.

Red onion relish

12oz / 350g red onion, peeled and finely chopped

4oz / 100g tomato, skinned and chopped

1oz / 25g demerara sugar

2 fl.oz / 50ml light malt vinegar

1/2 teaspoon tabasco sauce

1/4 teaspoon paprika

black pepper

Put all ingredients in a saucepan and stir well. Bring to the boil and simmer uncovered for about 20 minutes, until the mixture is reduced and thickens. Stir frequently to prevent sticking. Pour into a bowl, cover and refrigerate.

Truffle pudding *Serves 8*

6oz / 175g currants, chopped

4oz / 100g dried dates, finely chopped

4oz / 100g glacé cherries, washed, dried and chopped

4oz / 100g carob block, broken

3oz / 75g digestive biscuits, crushed

3oz / 75g cornflakes, crushed

2oz / 50g ground almonds

1oz / 25g sunflower margarine

2 tablespoons carob spread

2 tablespoons brandy

1 tablespoon maple syrup

1 teaspoon ground mixed spice

to finish

2oz / 50g carob block, broken

to serve

soya yoghurt or vegan ice cream

Put the 4oz / 100g carob block in a double boiler with the margarine, carob spread and maple syrup. Heat gently until melted, pour in the brandy and stir until smooth. Remove from the heat and add the remaining ingredients. Mix thoroughly and spoon the mixture into a $1^1/_2$ pint / 900ml pudding basin. Press each spoonful down firmly. Cover loosely with cling film and fit a flat saucer or round lid on the pudding inside the rim of the basin, with a heavy weight on top to push the pudding down. Keep in the fridge overnight. Loosen with a sharp knife and invert onto a plate. Melt the 2oz / 50g carob block in a double boiler and spread this evenly over the pudding. Put back in the fridge until set. Transfer to a serving plate, cut into wedges and serve with soya yoghurt or vegan ice cream.

NOVEMBER

Special occasions:

World Vegan Day (November 1)

Bonfire Night (November 5)

Martinmas (November 11)

Thanksgiving (USA: fourth Thursday)

St Andrew's Day (November 30)

Gaelic Night

Grapefruit, date and ginger cups

•

Mixed nut and lentil roast

Mushroom and brandy sauce

Jacket potatoes

Celeriac and apple purée

Baked red cabbage with raisins

Kumquat and sultana relish

•

Festive trifles

Grapefruit, date and ginger cups

2 grapefruit

demerara sugar

8 dessert dates, stoned and sliced

2 x 1 inch / 2.5cm pieces of stem ginger, sliced

shredded lettuce leaves

chopped walnuts

Cut the grapefruit in half and carefully cut out the segments. Remove the membrane from the segments and any that is left in the shells. Chop the segments and place in a bowl, sweeten with a little demerara sugar. Add the sliced dates and ginger and mix. Put some shredded lettuce in the bottom of each grapefruit shell. Drain the grapefruit mixture and divide between the shells. Sprinkle the tops with some chopped walnuts.

Mixed nut and lentil roast

6oz / 175g mixed nuts, ground

6oz / 175g brown lentils

4oz / 100g celery, trimmed and finely chopped

4oz / 100g carrot, scraped and grated

4oz / 100g fresh wholemeal breadcrumbs

1oz / 25g soya flour

1 onion, peeled and finely chopped

2 garlic cloves, crushed

1 tablespoon sunflower oil

1 tablespoon sherry

1 dessertspoon soy sauce

1 rounded teaspoon paprika

1 rounded teaspoon chives ·

black pepper

1 tablespoon flaked almonds

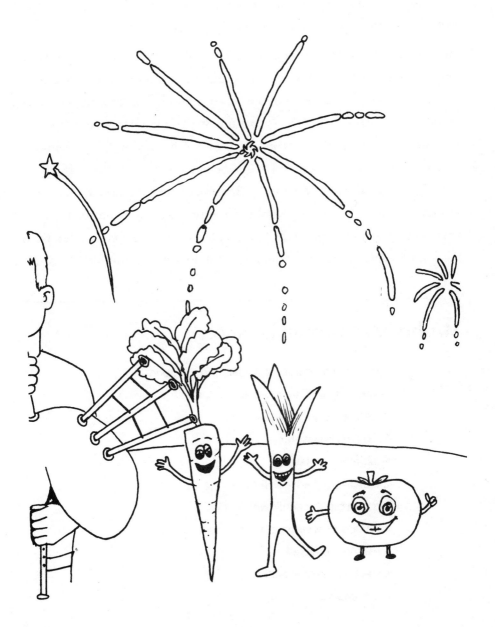

Cook the lentils until soft. Drain in a fine sieve, pressing out any excess water with the back of a spoon. Mash the lentils and set aside.

Heat the oil in a large saucepan and gently fry the celery, onion and garlic until softened. Remove from the heat and add the mashed lentils and all remaining ingredients apart from the flaked almonds. Mix thoroughly. Base-line and grease an 8 inch / 20cm loaf tin. Sprinkle the flaked almonds over the base. Spoon the mixture evenly into the tin, pressing down firmly with the back of a spoon. Cover with foil and bake in a preheated oven at 180°C / 350°F / Gas mark 4 for 45 minutes. Remove the foil and bake for a further 30 minutes. Run a sharp knife around the tin and invert the roast onto a baking tray. Carefully remove the base lining and neaten the edges. Return to the oven for approximately 10 minutes until golden. Cut into thick slices.

Mushroom and brandy sauce

4oz / 100g mushrooms, wiped and chopped

4 spring onions, trimmed and sliced

1 garlic clove, crushed

6 fl.oz / 175ml water

2 tablespoons brandy

2 tablespoons soya milk

1 dessertspoon sunflower oil

1 rounded dessertspoon cornflour

1 teaspoon parsley

1/4 teaspoon yeast extract

black pepper

Heat the oil in a saucepan and fry the onion and garlic until soft. Add the mushrooms and cook until the juices begin to run. Add the water, parsley and yeast extract and season with black pepper. Bring to the boil, cover and simmer for 5 minutes. Allow to cool, then liquidise until smooth. Pass through a sieve into a clean pan. Blend the cornflour with the brandy and soya milk. Add to the sauce and stir well. Bring to the boil whilst stirring and continue stirring until the sauce thickens.

Jacket potatoes

>4 large potatoes, each weighing 8-10oz / 225-300g
>sunflower oil

Scrub the potatoes, then using a sharp knife make a cross on the top of each one. Brush the potatoes with sunflower oil and transfer to a baking tin. Cover with foil and bake in a preheated oven at 200°C / 400°F / Gas mark 6 for approximately $1^1/_4$ hours until done. Turn once during cooking.

Celeriac and apple purée

>1lb / 450g celeriac, peeled and chopped
>12oz / 350g cooking apple, peeled, cored and chopped
>1 dessertspoon lemon juice
>1 rounded dessertspoon vegan margarine
>$^1/_4$ teaspoon ground cinnamon
>black pepper

Put the apple, lemon juice and ground cinnamon in a saucepan and cook gently until the apple is soft. Boil the celeriac until tender, drain and dry off over a low heat. Put in a blender with the cooked apple and margarine, season with black pepper and blend until smooth. Spoon into a serving bowl, cover with foil and place in a preheated oven at 180°C / 350°F / Gas mark 4 for about 15 minutes to heat through.

Baked red cabbage with raisins

12oz / 350g red cabbage, finely shredded

2oz / 50g raisins

1 onion, peeled and finely chopped

1 tablespoon red wine vinegar

1 tablespoon red wine

1 dessertspoon sunflower oil

1 teaspoon black mustard seeds

1/2 teaspoon ground allspice

vegan margarine

Heat the oil and gently fry the onion for 5 minutes. Put the cabbage in a pan of boiling water and blanch for 2 minutes. Drain well, add the onion and the remaining ingredients except the margarine, and mix thoroughly. Transfer to a casserole dish and dot the top with margarine. Cover tightly with foil and bake in a preheated oven at 170°C / 325F / Gas mark 3 for 30 minutes.

Kumquat and sultana relish

6oz / 175g kumquats, finely sliced

1oz / 25g sultanas

1oz / 25g demerara sugar

1 small onion, peeled and finely chopped

2 fl.oz / 50ml white wine vinegar

1 fl.oz / 25ml fresh orange juice

1/4 teaspoon ground mace

1/4 teaspoon ground coriander

Put the onion in a saucepan with the vinegar and orange juice. Bring to the boil, cover and simmer for 5 minutes. Remove from the heat and add the remaining ingredients. Stir well, again bring to the boil and simmer uncovered for about 15 minutes until the mixture is thick. Stir frequently to prevent sticking. Spoon into a serving bowl, cover and keep in the fridge until cold.

Festive trifles

8oz / 225g vegan fruit cake, chopped

8 fl.oz / 225ml tangerine drink (made with tangerine fruit syrup)

$1/2$ teaspoon agar agar

8 fl.oz / 225ml soya milk

2 tablespoons brandy

1 rounded tablespoon custard powder

1 rounded dessertspoon light muscovado sugar

toasted flaked almonds

4 glacé cherries

Divide the fruit cake between four sundae glasses. Dissolve the agar agar in the tangerine drink and heat whilst stirring until just below boiling point. Pour over the cake and allow to cool, then cover and refrigerate until set.

Pour the soya milk and brandy into a double boiler and add the custard powder and sugar. Stir until dissolved. Bring to the boil whilst stirring and continue stirring until the custard thickens. Pour over the cake and jelly. When cool, cover and chill for a few hours until cold and set. Before serving, sprinkle flaked almonds on each trifle and place a glacé cherry on top.

DECEMBER

Party suggestions:

Winter Solstice (December 22)

Christmas (December 25)

Boxing Day (December 26)

New Year's Eve (December 31)

Christmas Lunch

Red onion and wine soup

•

Christmas cracker

Roast potatoes

Mixed vegetables in cashew sauce

Brussels sprouts and leek purée

Cranberry and orange sauce

•

Christmas pudding

Red onion and wine soup

>1¼ lb / 550g red onions, peeled and chopped
>
>4oz / 100g potato, scraped and diced
>
>1 tablespoon olive oil
>
>20 fl.oz / 600ml water
>
>4 fl.oz / 125ml red wine
>
>1 teaspoon herbes du Provence
>
>black pepper

Heat the oil in a large saucepan and fry the onion until softened. Add the remaining ingredients and stir well. Bring to the boil, cover and simmer for 25 minutes until the vegetables are tender. Allow to cool slightly, then liquidise until smooth. Return to the cleaned pan and reheat whilst stirring.

Christmas cracker *Serves 6*

>9oz / 250g puff pastry
>
>*filling*
>
>4oz / 100g shelled chestnuts, grated
>
>4oz / 100g leek, finely shredded
>
>4oz / 100g carrot, scraped and grated
>
>2oz / 50g brazil nuts, grated
>
>2oz / 50g dried apricots, finely chopped
>
>2oz / 50g bulgar wheat
>
>1oz / 25g sunflower seeds, chopped
>
>1oz / 25g sultanas, chopped
>
>½ oz / 15g soya flour
>
>4 fl.oz / 125ml boiling water
>
>1 rounded tablespoon light tahini
>
>1 tablespoon sunflower oil
>
>1 tablespoon sherry

1 dessertspoon soy sauce

1 teaspoon yeast extract

1/2 teaspoon ground coriander

1/2 teaspoon paprika

1/4 teaspoon ground cinnamon

black pepper

soya milk

Dissolve the yeast extract and soy sauce in the boiling water. Add the bulgar wheat and leave for 10 minutes. Heat the oil in a large saucepan and gently fry the carrot and leek for a few minutes. Add the coriander, paprika and cinnamon and stir around for a few seconds. Remove from the heat. Drain the bulgar in a sieve over a bowl and press out any remaining liquid. Add the bulgar to the saucepan together with the chestnuts, brazil nuts, apricots, sunflower seeds and sultanas. Mix the sherry, soya flour and tahini with the bulgar liquid until smooth. Add to the filling mixture and season with black pepper. Combine thoroughly and set aside.

Roll out the pastry on a floured board to an oblong measuring 14 x 12 inches / 35 x 30cm. Cut out small triangles from the edges of the 12 inch / 30cm sides and keep these for decoration. Spoon the filling along the centre of the pastry to within 2 inches / 5cm of the serrated sides. Fold the long sides of the pastry over to enclose the filling and transfer the roll with the join underneath to a greased baking sheet. Pinch in 2 inches / 5cm from each end to make a cracker shape. Brush the top with soya milk and decorate with the triangles of pastry. Score the words 'Merry Xmas' on the top with a sharp knife and prick the pastry in a few places with a fork. Bake in a preheated oven at 170°C / 325°F / Gas mark 3 for 35-40 minutes until golden brown.

Roast potatoes

>
> 2lb / 900g potatoes, peeled
>
> vegetable oil

Cut the potatoes into even-sized chunks and boil for 5 minutes. Heat a little vegetable oil in a roasting tin in the oven, preheated at 200°C / 400°F / Gas mark 6. Drain the potatoes and put in the roasting tin. Spoon some of the hot oil over the potatoes and bake them for about 1 hour until golden, turning them occasionally during cooking to ensure even browning. Drain on kitchen paper before serving.

Mixed vegetables in cashew sauce

>
> 1lb / 450g prepared vegetables (e.g. a mixture of courgette, broccoli, celery, carrot, mushroom, parsnip, pepper), chopped
>
> 1 onion, peeled and finely chopped
>
> 1 tablespoon sunflower oil
>
> 8 fl.oz / 225ml water
>
> black pepper
>
> 1/2 teaspoon yeast extract
>
> 1oz / 25g cashew nuts, ground
>
> 1oz / 25g cashew nuts, halved and toasted
>
> 6 fl.oz / 175ml soya milk
>
> 2 dessertspoons cornflour

Heat the oil in a saucepan and gently fry the onion. Add the vegetables, water and yeast extract and bring to the boil. Cover and simmer gently until the vegetables are tender. (*Note:* some of the quicker cooking vegetables such as mushrooms can be added when the harder vegetables are almost cooked.)

Mix the ground cashews and cornflour with the soya milk and stir into the vegetables. Bring to the boil whilst stirring and continue stirring until the sauce thickens. Mix in half of the toasted cashew nuts. Transfer to a warmed serving dish and garnish with the remaining cashew nuts.

Brussels sprouts and leek purée

1lb / 450g Brussels sprouts

8oz / 225g leek, trimmed and sliced

1 teaspoon parsley

$1/2$ teaspoon yeast extract

black pepper

Remove the outer leaves from the sprouts. Cut the sprouts into quarters and steam them with the leek until tender. Transfer the vegetables to a blender. Dissolve the yeast extract in four tablespoonfuls of the steaming water. Add to the blender together with the parsley. Season with black pepper and blend. Spoon the mixture into a serving dish and cover with foil. Place in a preheated oven at 180°C / 350°F / Gas mark 4 for about 15 minutes until heated through.

Cranberry and orange sauce

8oz / 225g fresh cranberries

juice and finely grated rind of 1 orange

3 fl.oz / 75ml light malt vinegar

2oz / 50g light soft brown sugar

Put the cranberries, juice and grated rind and vinegar in a saucepan. Stir well and bring to the boil. Simmer gently until the cranberries burst. Remove from the heat and stir in the sugar. Return to the heat and simmer gently, stirring frequently, until the mixture thickens. Pour into a serving dish, cover and chill before serving.

Christmas pudding　*Makes 2 x 1¹/₄lb / 550g puddings*

These puddings can be made up to 4 weeks before Christmas and stored in the bottom of the fridge. If you want to flame the pudding, warm 2–3 table-spoonfuls of brandy in a small saucepan, pour over the hot pudding and set light to it immediately.

> 6oz / 175g cooking apple, peeled, cored and grated
>
> 4oz / 100g fine wholemeal self raising flour
>
> 4oz / 100g fresh wholemeal breadcrumbs
>
> 4oz / 100g currants
>
> 4oz / 100g raisins
>
> 4oz / 100g sultanas
>
> 4oz / 100g dried dates, finely chopped
>
> 2oz / 50g cut mixed peel
>
> 1oz / 25g mixed nuts, finely chopped
>
> 1oz / 25g dark molasses sugar
>
> 1oz / 25g soya flour
>
> 2 fl.oz / 50ml sunflower oil
>
> 2 tablespoons brandy
>
> juice and finely grated peel of 1 lemon
>
> 1 rounded tablespoon molasses
>
> 6 tablespoons water
>
> 1 rounded dessertspoon ground mixed spice

Put the water, soya flour, sunflower oil, brandy and molasses in a large bowl and stir well until smooth. Add the remaining ingredients and mix thoroughly. Divide the mixture between two ³/₄ pint / 450ml greased pudding basins. Cover the tops with a double layer of greaseproof paper. Tie foil securely over the top of the basins and steam the puddings for 3 hours. Keep the water topped up to ³/₄ the height of the pudding bowls. Once cooled, store in the fridge. Steam the puddings for 1¹/₂ hours before serving.

INDEX

Starters

Main courses

Vegetable dishes

Sauces

Relishes

Desserts